CRAFTING WITH PAPIER-MÂCHÉ

By Dana Meachen Rau
Illustrated by Kathleen Petelinsek

CHERRY LAKE PUBLISHING • ANN ARBOR, MICHIGAN

CHERRY
LAKE
Publishing

Published in the United States of America by Cherry Lake Publishing
Ann Arbor, Michigan
www.cherrylakepublishing.com

Photo Credits: Page 4, © science photo/Shutterstock.com; page 5, ©
Emilio Pastor de Miguel/Shutterstock.com; page 29, © Andrew Olscher/
Shutterstock.com.

Library of Congress Cataloging-in-Publication Data
 Rau, Dana Meachen, 1971– author.
 Crafting with papier-mâché / by Dana Meachen Rau.
 pages cm. — (Crafts) (How-to library)
 Summary: "Learn how to create a variety of fun papier-mache crafts
with the detailed step-by-step instructions in this book" — Provided by
publisher.
 Audience: Grades 4–6.
 Includes bibliographical references and index.
 ISBN 978-1-63362-367-5 (lib. bdg.) — ISBN 978-1-63362-395-8 (pbk.)
— ISBN 978-1-63362-423-8 (pdf) —ISBN 978-1-63362-451-1 (e-book)
 1. Papier-mâché--Juvenile literature. 2. Handicraft—Juvenile literature. I.
Title. II. Series: How-to library.

 TT871.R38 2016
 745.54'2—dc23   2014048016

Cherry Lake Publishing would like to acknowledge the work of The
Partnership for 21st Century Skills. Please visit www.p21.org for more
information.

Printed in the United States of America
Corporate Graphics
July 2015

A NOTE TO ADULTS:
Please review the instructions
for these craft projects before
your children make them. Be
sure to help them with any
steps you do not think they can
safely do on their own.

A NOTE TO KIDS:
Be sure to ask an adult
for help with these
craft activities when you
need it. Always put your
safety first!

TABLE OF CONTENTS

Style and Tradition

Newspaper is a common ingredient in papier-mâché.

Don't throw that newspaper away. Don't even put it in the recycling bin. You can turn it into a beautiful sculpture!

Papier-mâché (pronounced PAY-per ma-SHAY) is the process of soaking paper in some sort of **adhesive**, and then laying it over a mold or form to make an object or piece of art. People have been making papier-mâché for centuries.

Paper was invented in China during the Han Dynasty, which lasted from 206 BCE to 220 CE. Papier-mâché was invented during the same period. One of its earliest uses was to make helmets for soldiers. In China and Japan, artists also used it to make a variety of decorative items. Objects made from papier-mâché were both lightweight and strong, thanks to layers of **lacquer**.

As countries traded goods with each other, the use of papier-mâché spread throughout the world. By the 18th century, craftspeople in England and France were producing many papier-mâché items. They used papier-mâché to decorate walls and ceilings. They also used it to make boxes, trays, chairs, and even larger items such as beds and bookcases. As the craft spread from Asia to Europe to America, different cultures developed their own papier-mâché styles and traditions.

With some very simple ingredients, a few bright ideas, and your own style, you can make unique papier-mâché pieces, too!

Detailed sculptures can be made of papier-mâché!

Basic Tools

Making things out of papier-mâché is a lot of fun. However, it can take awhile. One of the most important supplies you'll need is time! It will take about five to six days to make each project in this book. Plan ahead if you need a project completed by a certain time. Here are some other supplies you will need:

Mold Supplies (see pages 8–9)

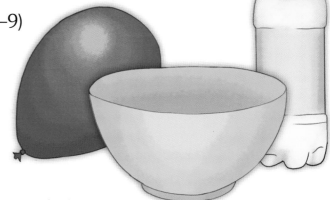

- Balloons
- Bowls
- Bottles
- Plastic wrap
- Plastic drinking straws

Framework Supplies (see pages 8–9)

- A variety of cardboard shapes, such as shoe boxes, cereal boxes, paper towel rolls, and toilet paper rolls
- Aluminum foil
- Plastic cups
- Masking tape

Papier-Mâché Supplies (see pages 10–12)

- Apron
- Flour
- Water
- Measuring cups
- Bowl
- Whisk
- Lots of newspapers
- Ruler
- Scissors

Pedestal Supplies (see page 12)

- Plastic containers of various sizes
- Plastic cups
- Tall vases
- Skewers
- Foam blocks

Decorating and Painting Supplies (see page 13)

- Sponge brushes
- Paintbrushes
- Paper plate palette
- Acrylic paint
- Tissue paper
- Permanent markers
- Paint pens
- Polycrylic
- White glue
- Ribbon
- Craft felt
- Craft foam
- Glitter

Cleaning Tips

Even though papier-mâché is a messy process, try to keep yourself and your workspace as clean as you can. Wear an apron. Cover your workspace with newspaper or a washable tablecloth. Work in a kitchen if possible, so you can be near a sink to rinse your hands. Because papier-mâché paste is made of flour and water, it washes off easily with warm soapy water. If you can, clean up while the paste is still wet. It is harder to clean up after it dries.

Molds and Frameworks

There are two ways to make papier-mâché sculptures. One way is to use a mold that you remove when you are finished forming your piece. The other is to build a framework that will support your piece from the inside and stay in place when you are done.

To use a mold

Cover your mold, such as a bowl or bottle, with a layer of plastic wrap. This will make it easier to remove from the sculpture after it dries. To remove a balloon from your finished piece, hold the mouth of the balloon and snip a hole in it with scissors. When it pops, it will pull away from the sides of the sculpture. Gently pull it out of your piece.

To make a framework

Look at all of your framework supplies to decide which will provide the best support for your project. Then cut them into the right shapes and tape them together as needed.

If you need shapes with defined edges, you may want to use boxes. If you need legs, arms, or other **cylinders**, paper towel or toilet paper tubes might be best. Aluminum foil is easy to mold into any shape you want.

Use masking tape to hold your framework pieces together. It doesn't matter if the framework looks a little messy. It will be covered by papier-mâché. It is more important to make it sturdy. The framework acts like the skeleton in your body—it helps your sculpture stand up and keep its shape.

The Papier-Mâché Process

You will need to follow these basic steps for all of the projects in this book.

Step One
Make the Papier-Mâché Paste
This is the glue that will hold your project together. So put on your apron and whip up a batch!

Measure 1 cup (237 milliliters) of flour and 1.5 cups (355 mL) of water into a large bowl. Whisk them together until your mixture is thick but still runny, without any lumps. Add a little more flour or water as needed to get the perfect **consistency**.

Step Two
Prepare Your Mold or Framework
See pages 8 and 9 to learn how to prepare your mold or build your framework.

You can save leftover paste in an airtight container in the refrigerator.

Step Three
Lay on the Layers

1. Tear a whole bunch of newspapers into strips. (Tearing is better than cutting. Rough edges will dry smoother than straight edges.) For most projects, you should try to make the strips about 1 inch (2.5 centimeters) wide. If you are working with a smaller mold or framework, you might want to use thinner, shorter strips. This will make it easier to wrap them around your piece.

2. Dip a strip of newspaper into your bowl of paste. Hold it up with one hand. Place two fingers of your other hand on either side of the strip and run them down the strip from top to bottom (over the bowl) so the extra paste drips off.

3. Lay the strip on top of your mold or structure and press it flat. Repeat this process with another strip, slightly overlapping the first one.

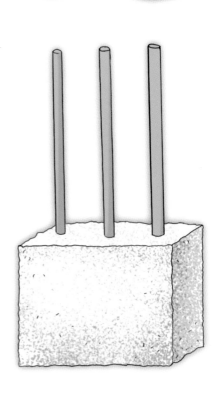

4. Continue dipping
and laying down strips,
overlapping in different directions, until
the entire mold or framework is covered.
5. Set your sculpture aside in a safe place
to dry overnight. Then clean up!
6. Repeat the process the next day. Set
your sculpture aside to dry again.
7. Repeat the process two more times so
you have four layers of paper in all.

Put It on a Pedestal!

It helps to lift your object up from your
workspace as you add layers of newspaper.
You can use plastic containers, plastic cups,
or skewers stuck in foam as **pedestals**,
depending on the project.

VERY IMPORTANT!
Let your sculpture dry
COMPLETELY between each
layer. Otherwise, it might get
moldy. If you live in a humid area,
you may have to wait more than a
day for each layer to dry.

Decorating and Painting Tips

Once your sculpture is completely dry, it is time to decorate. Paint adds color and detail to your sculpture. Use a paper plate as a **palette** to hold and mix paint colors. Sponge brushes are helpful for covering large areas with color. Smaller paintbrushes are good for details.

After you paint, you can add finer details with markers. If you are drawing over a light color of paint, permanent markers work best. If you are drawing over a dark color, you can use paint pens. Instead of painting, you can add color by using bits of colorful tissue paper as a final layer of papier-mâché.

Once the paint is dry, you can add a layer of polycrylic. Polycrylic is a clear substance that hardens to protect the project underneath. It looks cloudy when you paint it on, but it will dry clear.

WATER BASED

Polycrylic

Victorian Lacquer Bowl

Black lacquer papier-mâché bowls were popular during the Victorian era in England. They were decorated with natural images such as flowers and birds, and they were often accented with gold.

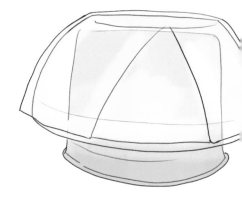

Materials

- Bowl and plastic wrap (for the mold)
- Plastic container (for the pedestal)
- 1-inch (2.5 cm) torn strips of newspaper
- Papier-mâché paste (see page 10)
- Scissors
- Black acrylic paint
- Gold leafing pen
- Paintbrush and sponge brush
- Paper plate palette
- Polycrylic

Steps

1. Cover the underside of the bowl very tightly with plastic wrap. Then place it on top of a plastic container to lift it up from your workspace.
2. Dip the newspaper strips in paste and lay them over the bowl. Continue overlapping strips until the surface is completely covered.

Let the sculpture dry overnight. Repeat this process on the following three days (or whenever each layer is totally dry).

3. On the fifth day, gently remove the bowl mold and plastic wrap from your papier-mâché bowl. Use scissors to trim the ragged edges.

4. With a paintbrush, paint the inside of the bowl with black paint. Once the paint is dry, flip the bowl over and paint the underside. Let it dry. Draw flowery details with the gold leafing pen on the inside and outside of the bowl. Once again, let it dry completely.

5. With a sponge brush, add a layer of polycrylic on the inside of the bowl. After it dries, flip the bowl over and paint polycrylic on the underside. Let it dry completely.

NOTE: This bowl is decorative. It is not meant to hold food or be washed!

Anytime Ornaments

Ornaments are fun to hang on a Christmas tree, from a ceiling, or anywhere you need a bit of decoration! Use a variety of colored tissue paper to decorate these ornaments, depending on the holiday. Make a red, white, and blue ornament for Independence Day or a green one for St. Patrick's Day!

Materials

- Small round balloon, such as the type used for water balloons (for the mold)
- Small cup (for the pedestal)
- 0.5-inch (1.3 cm) torn strips of newspaper
- Papier-mâché paste (see page 10)
- Polycrylic
- Colored tissue paper, ripped into small squares
- Sponge brush
- Skewer and foam block (for a pedestal)
- Craft foam
- Scissors
- 12-inch (30.5 cm) length of ribbon

Steps

1. Blow up a balloon. Set it on the cup. Dip newspaper strips in paste and lay them over the balloon. Continue

overlapping strips until the surface is completely covered. Let the ornament dry overnight. Every so often, change the position of the balloon so it doesn't stick to the cup. Repeat the process on the next three days (or whenever each layer is totally dry). On the fifth day, remove the balloon.

2. Brush a little polycrylic onto your ornament and lay a piece of tissue paper on top. Continue painting small areas and adding tissue paper until the ornament is covered. Then paint polycrylic over the whole surface. Set the ornament on the skewer and foam pedestal until it dries completely.

3. To prepare your ornament for hanging, cut a 1-inch (2.5 cm) circle out of the craft foam. Fold the circle in half and cut two small slits into the folded edge. Thread the ends of the ribbon into the two slits and pull them all the way through. Knot the ends of the ribbon to form a loop.

4. Fold the foam circle and poke it into the hole in the ornament. You can use your finger or a pencil if needed. Once it is inside, it will unfold to keep the ribbon from coming out.

Birthday Cake

Surprise a friend or family member with this fake birthday cake. Hide a present underneath, then lift the cake to reveal the gift. Start a new birthday tradition by using the cake again and again!

Materials

- Shoe box (for the framework)
- Plastic container (for the pedestal)
- 1-inch (2.5 cm) torn strips of newspaper
- Papier-mâché paste (see page 10)
- Waxed paper
- Cookie sheet
- 10 to 12 plastic drinking straws
- Masking tape
- 0.5-inch (1.3 cm) cut strips of newspaper
- Two colors of acrylic paint
- Sponge brushes and paintbrushes
- Paper plate palette
- White glue
- Polycrylic

Steps

1. Set your box onto the container. Dip the wider newspaper strips in paste and lay them over the bottom of the box. Next, place strips along the sides and bottom of the box. Fold the ends up and under the box's open edge. Overlap strips until the box is completely covered.

2. Lift the box from the pedestal and set it on a piece of waxed paper. Let it dry overnight. (If you leave the box on the container, it might **distort** the box as it dries.) Repeat the papier-mâché process three more times as the layers dry.

3. Next, you can make accent decorations. Place a piece of waxed paper on a cookie sheet. Tape the straws onto the waxed paper with a little space between each one. Lay the thinner strips of dipped newspaper across them. Gently push down the strips between each straw. Let them dry overnight.

4. Gently remove the dried strips from the straws. Use a paintbrush to paint them with acrylic paint. Use a sponge brush to paint the box on all sides with your other color. Let them dry.

5. Time to decorate the cake! Paint flower details and the words "Happy Birthday" on the top side. Then add strips of glue along the edges. Place your accent decorations on the glue and press down on the low parts. Cut and piece together these strips as needed.

6. Once the glue is dry, add a layer of polycrylic on all of the surfaces. Let it dry.

Flashy Flamingo

Create a little tropical flair with this glitzy flamingo.

Materials

- Aluminum foil, paper towel tube, ice cream carton, cardboard (for the framework)
- Masking tape
- Stapler
- Vase (for the pedestal)
- 1-inch (2.5 cm) torn strips of newspaper
- Papier-mâché paste (see page 10)
- Sponge brushes and paintbrushes
- Pink, white, and black acrylic paint
- Paper plate palette
- Black permanent marker
- Polycrylic
- Glitter
- 18- to 24-inch (46 to 61 cm) wooden dowel
- Duct tape

Steps

1. Mold the aluminum foil into a horseshoe shape. Squeeze one of the ends to make it pointy. This will be your flamingo's beak. Stick the other end of the foil into the end of the paper towel tube and use masking tape to tape it in place. Tape around the flamingo's head to smooth out bumps.

2. Place the tube on the end of the ice cream carton. Slip the stapler inside the tube and staple it to the carton as high as you can. Then staple the tube flat at the bottom. Cut a fan shape from cardboard. Tape it to the other end of the carton. **Reinforce** all of the pieces with plenty of tape.

3. Place your flamingo onto the vase pedestal. Dip the newspaper strips in paste and wrap them around the flamingo form. Overlap strips until everything is completely covered. Let it dry overnight. Repeat the process three more times.

4. After the fourth layer has dried, paint your flamingo pink. Let the paint dry for about an hour. Then paint around the flamingo's eye and half of its beak white. Add wings on its sides and feather lines on its tail, too. Paint the tip of its beak black. Let the paint dry. Then draw the eyes and beak lines.

5. Squeeze polycrylic onto your palette and add glitter. Stir it with the sponge brush, and then paint it onto your flamingo. Let the polycrylic dry completely.

6. Use duct tape to attach the dowel to the inside front of the flamingo's body. Stick the other end of the dowel into the dirt of a potted plant to display your flamingo.

No-Care Cactus

Houseplants need a lot of care and attention. Even cactuses need some water. But you don't have to worry about remembering to water this papier-mâché cactus!

Materials

- 2 toilet paper tubes, 1 paper towel tube, aluminum foil (for the framework)
- Scissors
- Masking tape
- Skewer and foam block (for the pedestal)
- 1-inch (2.5 cm) torn strips of newspaper
- Papier-mâché paste (see page 10)

- Light green, dark green, and white acrylic paint
- Sponge brushes and paintbrushes
- Paper plate palette
- Polycrylic
- Small terra-cotta pot
- Small stones

Steps

1. Measure down about 1 inch (2.5 cm) from the end of one toilet paper tube, then cut a slit almost all the way across it. Bend back the end that is still attached to form an L shape. Place tape inside and outside of the tube to hold it in place. Repeat with the other toilet paper tube.

Tape the two toilet paper tubes onto opposite sides of the paper towel tube to make a cactus shape. Place the cactus form upside down onto the skewer-and-foam pedestal.

2. Dip the newspaper strips in paste and lay them over the cactus. Gravity will help your cactus's arms hang straight down as you work. Overlap strips until the surface is completely covered. Let it dry overnight.

3. Flip the dried cactus upright on the skewer. Scrunch up pieces of aluminum foil and stuff them into the open ends of the tubes. Add the next layer of dipped newspaper strips to completely cover the form. Let it dry. Repeat the process two more times.

4. Once the fourth layer is dry, paint your cactus light green. Put it on the pedestal and let the paint dry. Paint lines on your cactus in dark green. Let the paint dry. Add white spikes along the green lines. Let it dry.

5. Add a layer of polycrylic and let it dry completely. To display your cactus, stick the bottom end into the pot. Surround it with stones to hold it in place.

Surprise Rabbit Puppet

This project is made of multiple pieces—a top hat, a rabbit head, and paws. Put them together and—abracadabra!—you have a fun magic trick.

Materials for the Top Hat

- Two cereal boxes (for the framework)
- Scissors
- Masking tape
- Pencil
- Ruler
- 1-inch (2.5 cm) torn strips of newspaper
- Papier-mâché paste (see page 10)
- Waxed paper
- Black acrylic paint
- Sponge brushes and paintbrushes
- Paper plate palette
- Polycrylic
- Two sheets of craft felt
- White glue

Steps

1. Cut the front and back sides from the cereal boxes. Tape the ends of two of these pieces together to make a large cylinder. This is the tall part of the hat.

Trace one end of the cylinder onto another of the cereal box sides. Then draw a larger circle about 2 inches (5 cm) out from the first one. Cut out the outer and inner circles, leaving a ring of cardboard. This is the brim of the hat. Tape it to the tall part of the hat.

2. Set the hat on your workspace so the brim is on top. Dip a newspaper strip into paste. Start a strip on the inside of the hat, then wrap it all the way over the brim and down the side of the cylinder. Continue until you have covered the whole brim. Then flip the hat over. Cover the cylinder with strips. Place the hat on waxed paper. Let it dry overnight. Repeat the process three more times as each layer dries.

3. Once the fourth layer is dry, paint the brim of the hat in black. When the paint is dry, flip the hat over and paint the rest of it. Let it dry. Then add a layer of polycrylic and let it dry completely.

4. Cut sheets of felt to fit the inside of the hat. Squeeze glue onto the backs of the felt pieces and place them into the hat. Push them as flat as you can against the sides.

Materials for the Rabbit

- Edges of the cereal boxes
  (for the paw and ear frameworks)
- Scissors
- Masking tape
- 0.5-inch (1.3 cm) torn strips of newspaper
- Papier-mâché paste (see page 10)
- Skewer and foam block (for the pedestal)
- Balloon (for the head mold)
- Plastic container (for the pedestal)
- White and pink acrylic paint
- Paper plate palette
- Sponge brushes and paintbrushes
- Black permanent marker
- Polycrylic
- An old glove

Steps for the Rabbit

1. For the paws, cut out two pieces of
   cardboard each measuring 2 inches by
   4 inches (5 cm by 10 cm). Fold each piece
   in half and tape the sides closed. Then bend
   them so that your thumb and middle
   finger can fit comfortably into each one.
2. Dip the newspaper strips into paste
   and wrap them around the paws.

Place them on the skewer-and-foam pedestal. Repeat the process three more times as each layer dries.

3. For the rabbit's head, blow up the balloon to a **diameter** of about 4 inches (10 cm). Make sure it can fit inside the top hat with extra room around it. Set it down on the container pedestal. Dip the newspaper strips into paste and lay them over the balloon. Continue overlapping strips until the surface is completely covered. Let it dry overnight. Every so often, change the position of the balloon so it doesn't stick to the pedestal.

4. Once the first layer is dry, cut out two ear shapes from the cardboard. Tape them onto the top of your rabbit's head. Cover the ears and the rest of the head with a layer of dipped newspaper strips. The ears may flop down from the weight of the paste. When you set the rabbit aside to dry, place it upside down so the ears sit in the position you want. After they have dried in place, you can turn the head to dry the underside.

5. Repeat the papier-mâché process two more times as each layer dries. Once the fourth layer is dry, remove the balloon. Make sure your index finger fits comfortably into the hole. If it is too tight, cut it wider with scissors.

6. Paint the head and the two paws white. Let dry. Add a pink nose, pink ear shapes, and pink paws. Let the paint dry. Use a marker to outline the pink areas and then draw eyes and a mouth. Add a layer of polycrylic and let it dry completely before putting everything together.

Putting It All Together

Place your hand into the glove. Then place the head onto your index finger and the paws onto your thumb and middle finger. Hide the puppet inside the hat, say "abracadabra," and pop the rabbit out from the top!

Endless Ideas

Once you start working with the papier-mâché projects in this book, your creative mind will probably explode with more ways to use your new skills.

- Make a bunch of pet rocks and start a rock band.
- Make a whole zoo of animals.
- Make furniture for your dolls or stuffed animals.
- Make a mobile of planets and hang it from your ceiling.
- Make a cityscape filled with skyscrapers, cars, and people.
- Make anything you can imagine!

There is no limit to what you can make with the simple ingredients of newspaper, flour, water, and creativity!

Some papier-mâché projects can look good enough to eat!

Glossary

adhesive (ad-HEE-siv) a substance that makes two things stick together

consistency (kuhn-SIS-tuhn-see) the thickness of a substance

cylinders (SIL-un-durz) shapes with flat, circular ends and sides shaped like the outside of a tube

diameter (dye-AM-i-tur) a straight line through the center of a circle, connecting opposite sides

distort (dis-TORT) to twist out of the normal shape

humid (HYOO-mid) moist and usually very warm

lacquer (LACK-ur) a substance that forms a clear, protective layer

palette (PAL-it) a flat surface used for mixing paints

pedestals (PED-i-stuhlz) bases or supports

reinforce (ree-in-FORS) to make something stronger or more effective

For More Information

Books

Good, Jonni. *How to Make Masks!* La Grande, OR: Wet Cat Books, 2012.

Henry, Sally, and Trevor Cook. *Papier-Mâché.* New York: PowerKids Press, 2011.

Jocelyn, Marthe. *Sneaky Art: Crafty Surprises to Hide in Plain Sight.* Somerville, MA: Candlewick Press, 2013.

Jones, Jen. *Cool Crafts with Newspapers, Magazines & Junk Mail: Green Projects for Resourceful Kids.* Mankato, MN: Capstone Press, 2011.

Terry, Kayte. *Paper Made! 101 Exceptional Projects to Make Out of Everyday Paper.* New York: Workman Publishing, 2012.

Web Sites

About.com: Papier Mâché Projects and How-Tos

http://familycrafts.about.com/od/papermache/

Visit this site for advice, paste recipes, and papier-mâché project ideas.

Enchanted Learning: Papier-Mâché Crafts

www.enchantedlearning.com/crafts/papiermache/

Find lots of craft ideas at this fun site.

Free Kids Crafts: Recycled Paper Crafts

www.freekidscrafts.com/recycled-crafts/recycled-paper-crafts

This site is full of ideas for ways to craft with paper instead of throwing it away.

Ultimate Paper Mache

www.ultimatepapermache.com

This informative site is filled with tips and tutorials to help you along with your papier-mâché projects.

Index

About the Author

Dana Meachen Rau is the author of more than 300 books for children on many topics, including science, history, cooking, and crafts. She creates, experiments, researches, and writes from her home office in Burlington, Connecticut.